31 DAY CHALLENGE TO A

CHANGED YOU

An Intensive Guide for Personal Transformation

By Sadhvi Siddhali Shree

Siddha Sangh Publications

SIDDHA SANGH PUBLICATIONS

9985 E. Hwy 56

Windom, Texas, 75492

orders@siddhasanghpublications.com

ISBN 0-9843854-0-1

ISBN 978-0-9843854-0-9

LCCN 2009942982

Printed in the United States of America.

Disclaimer

Please note that not all exercises, diet plans or other suggestions, mentioned in this book are suitable for everyone. This book is not intended to replace the need for consultation with medical doctors and other professionals. Before changing any diet, exercise routine, or any other plans discussed in this book, seeks appropriate professional medical advice to ensure it is acceptable for you. The author and publisher are not responsible for any problems arising from the use or misuse of the information provided in this book.

Dedicated to Acharya Shree Yogeesh & Ms. R. –
for having confidence in me.

Table of Contents

Foreword

Sadhvi Siddhali Shree is a rising and shining star in the world of spiritual and social reformation. Within a short period of time after entering the monastic life, she already has begun to fulfill her purpose of changing herself and helping others. I am very proud of her accomplishments, like a father would be of his own child.

When I first met Siddhali Shree nearly six years ago, I saw her as the cure to human suffering and pain. She will uplift and bring new life to our current society, which is filled with negative people and lost souls. Like a shooting star on a clear dark night, she will give hope to the world.

Siddhali Shree's *31 Day Challenge to a Changed You,* is like honey: delicious and sweet. Although sweet, it will make a person feel alert and alive, like a bee sting.

I am confident that her suggested challenges will transform human life, purify the mind, and bring clarity to all thoughts. This book will bring focus to the scattered, wisdom to the debater, and motivation to the tensed.

Like Triveni Sangham of India, where the three major rivers meet, this book is a major center point for one to know the essence of human life, its real meaning, and qualities.

My Blessings to Sadhvi Siddhali Shree for her efforts towards helping humanity, as I know that this will be a life changing stepping stone in the life of those that read it and take up her *31 Day Challenge to a Changed You.*

Acharya Shree Yogeesh

Preface

I believe that everyone has the innate power and ability to change if they put effort in the right direction. I myself have made the commitment to change, know myself, and in the process hope to help others do the same.

Since I was seventeen, when I was first inspired to change my life, I have always wanted to write a book to help others discover what I had – true happiness, peace, and love. I was always reminded by my spiritual teacher, Acharya Shree Yogeesh, to wait until it was the "right time" to write. When it is the "right time", he said it would "just flow with little effort." After years of impatience and letting go of the idea of writing, the idea to create this "Book for Change" came about.

A few weeks ago, I was considering some ideas of how to continue my discipline towards personal change on a daily basis. Two years ago, my spiritual teacher used to give me "Discipline for the Day" where he would give me specific things to do or not to do each day, to help me increase my awareness. I came up with the idea of writing my own "Discipline for the Day" and putting these simple disciplines on little sheets of paper, put them into a box, and on each day, perform the discipline. It was in a moment of reflection on how much I would change as a result of discipline, did the idea to write happen. The idea that inspired this entire book is actually the 31st challenge.

One simple thought led to the immediate listings of the possible challenges I would ask readers to perform. Then I began to add brief overviews on why such change is positive in their life, and the book began to take shape of its own. My original intention was to create an e-book to add to my personal spiritual blog, *SiddhaliShree.com*, but I felt that because this book would act as an opportunity to journal thoughts, it might as well be a paperback book to write in.

Less than one week after beginning my writings with only fourteen challenges completed, I had the fortunate blessing of Fayvor, a spiritual retreater who came for a Thanksgiving weekend retreat, to offer her time and effort in helping me edit this book. Because of her encouragement and ideas, I was inspired even more to finish this book. Not only was I inspired to finish, I also officially established Siddha Sangh Publications, a new publishing company dedicated to offering self improvement and spiritual books, video, and audio.

Only eighteen days ago did the idea to write a self improvement book happen and now two days before my 26th birthday I am writing this preface after having completed my writings. All I can say is that it really was just the "right time".

31 Day Challenge to a Changed You is only the beginning to my efforts to reach a worldwide audience in bringing about self and world change. I believe that once a person feels a spark to change themselves, they can, and will be able to transform. If I am able to help at least one person totally change their life, my life's purpose is complete. It is with hope that YOU are this person.

Change

Real change means to discover and transform yourself. Change is self discovery, because deep down you do not know who or what the real you is. It is beyond body and mind, health and wealth, name and fame. In order to discover who you are, you have to make changes that shed the layers of clouds that cover your eyes – it could be fears, anger, low self-esteem, personal issues, financial worries, and an endless list which are not you - yet you believe them to be you. Once these layers are removed, you are able to experience true happiness.

Change is also transformational because nothing in this universe is constant. The world is constantly changing, people are changing, and you are evolving daily. You know that seven days ago, you have somehow changed, yet you have remained the same. Change is growth.

This book is an intensive guide to help you peel away the layers of emotional, mental, and physical blocks that keep you from knowing yourself.

The Real You

To know the real you, you must first realize what you are not. Although you might have anger in your heart, you are not your anger. Although you might be wealthy or poor, you are not your money. Although you might have imperfect or perfect skin, you are not your body. The list can go on and on.

The real you is beyond emotion and mind and unaffected by pain and suffering. It is like a light which is very pure, innocent, and at peace. It is called the soul.

Because emotions and mind fluctuate from one moment to the next, we know that is not us. Like an ocean, once we dive deep beyond the splashing surface waves, we experience true calmness and peace. Our emotions and mind keep us from diving to the bottom of the real self.

The Need for Personal Transformation

Without changing our habits of identifying ourselves with our thoughts and feelings, we will constantly sway throughout life not ever experiencing true happiness. However, if we find ways to understand our feelings and nature of our mind, we can be less affected and bring true joy into our life.

Change is a process of knowing our true self. Without changing our habits, ideology, or the emotions we cling to, the layers of clouds will not dissolve. Change leads to inner truth and peace.

Process of Change

Change first begins with identification of a problem or issue – mental, emotional, or physical. Once you have awareness of the issue, then you will be able to take baby steps to help improve various aspects of your life. Remember, change is a gradual, but continual process.

Awareness to Change

Real change requires self-awareness, which is the ability to discern in an intense moment between right or wrong in order to transcend the moment. For example, if you are in an argument and you know you have a habit of using abusive language, before you say the bad word, you become aware and decide not to use such language because you know it can result in someone being hurt. Self-awareness is a pheno-menon that happens in a single moment. Change occurs, when self-awareness increases and is sustained throughout the day.

Excuses to Change

Change is often talked about at the beginning of the New Year because people want to start off their year with positive thinking and high goals. After a few days into the New Year a person may have given up on themselves because they realize it is very difficult to change. It is important to know the common excuses not to change, as they might arise in your own mind during your 31 days of challenges. Common excuses are:

Not enough time. Many are under the impression that change requires a lot of time, and they do not have it. Change does require time, but 2 - 5 minutes each day to dedicate towards a changed you, is not *too* time consuming.

Requires too much energy. Being lazy is only an excuse to deter you from achieving transformation. Change requires self discipline, effort, and passion. Energy should be put towards a better life and realizing true happiness.

Results are slow. Change is gradual and it is not necessary the fruits of your effort will show in an hour, the next day, or year. Real change is a lifetime of continuous effort because there is always something to change. Do not give up on yourself.

No inspiration or support. The most important person that needs to believe you can change is YOU. Many will resist your personal changes towards the good because deep down they feel they are unable to do it, so they may not show support for your new endeavors. Remember, change is for you and by you. You never know, you might inspire them to change, too!

Positive change is a sign of weakness. When you change yourself and your ways, you might fear that you become weak in the eyes of your family, friends, and society. Goodness does not equal weakness. Only the strong-willed and courageous are able to change and for this, you should be proud.

No need to change. Resistance to change arises because you refuse to accept that there are aspects of your life that need to be changed. Once the wall of resistance comes down, your eyes will open to many areas of your life that need improvement. Change happens when you are humble to yourself and others.

You have the power and ability to change yourself. By changing yourself you inspire others to change, too. Reading and completing each of the daily challenges will help you in different aspects of your life. Although this guide is very simple, it is also intense. It is designed to help you discover who you are, your purpose, areas of your life that need change, and how to change them.

Believe in yourself, because I believe in you.

About this Guide

This guide has been designed to help you change towards personal transformation in a simple, intensive, and disciplined way for the next 31 days of your life. The challenges vary in degree of difficulty, but stay committed and on track. You will see after 31 days how much you have grown.

Every morning read one daily challenge and complete the task before the day's end. If by chance you miss a day, continue where you left off.

The following are section descriptions that are in the challenge chapters.

Introduction of an Issue and Benefits of Change

Each daily challenge will include a brief overview of the problem, its effects on your life, and the benefits of changing it. This guide focuses on various issues such as: mental, emotional, health, environmental, financial, and societal.

Thoughts to Consider

Following the introduction, the *Thoughts to Consider* are several questions for you to reflect on before taking up your challenge. Real change cannot happen without getting to the root of the issue. These self reflective questions will guide you to finding the deeper answers and solutions to your problems.

Daily Challenge

To help you make a positive change towards an issue, you will be given a simple task to complete for the day. Most challenges require between 2 – 30 minutes of your time.

Weekly Challenge

After seven days of challenges you have the option to complete weekly tasks, which is another opportunity for self reflection.

Reflective Questions

Following the daily or weekly challenge, you will be given a set of reflective questions to answer through writing. This guide will also be a journal to record reflections, thoughts, experiences, and progress.

Day 1: Personal Changes

31 ways you would like to change.

Identifying what needs to be changed requires intense self reflection and soul searching. One of the most difficult things in life is finding your own personal weaknesses and admitting to yourself you have them. The reason for difficulty is because no one wants to appear weak or different. It is important to understand that there is no such thing as "normal". Everyone is uniquely talented and special within their own purpose of life. Furthermore, not a single human being is perfect. Everyone has their own flaws, weaknesses, mental, emotional, physical habits, and different upbringings.

Everyone, including you, has room for change on all levels of your life.

THOUGHTS TO CONSIDER

- What does happiness mean to you?
- What do you like and dislike about yourself?
- What areas of your life need improvement?
- Why do you want to change?
- What would you like to change mentally, emotionally, and physically?

Challenge: Reflect for 30 minutes and list 31 ways to change.

1. _____
2. _____
3. _____
4. _____
5. _____
6. _____
7. _____
8. _____
9. _____
10. _____
11. _____
12. _____
13. _____
14. _____
15. _____
16. _____
17. _____
18. _____
19. _____
20. _____
21. _____
22. _____
23. _____
24. _____
25. _____
26. _____
27. _____
28. _____
29. _____
30. _____
31. _____

Day 2: Me in the Mirror

Stare at your reflection in the mirror and discover who you are.

When you get ready for school, work, or just to get cleaned up, and fixing your hair, shaving, or putting on makeup, have you ever really thought about who the person is in the mirror? Do you even know this person?

We have become a society that promotes self identification with the body, but not identification with the true and inner self. Too many times we see both men and women suffering with pain and self-confidence issues because they are not accepting of their physical appearance. Remember, although it is important to take care of our bodies and be healthy, we are not this body.

You are that which is special, unique, and beautiful despite whether or not your body is "approved by society". You need to love yourself for who you are - beyond your body and mind. Loving yourself is a major step towards personal transformation.

THOUGHTS TO CONSIDER

- When you look into the mirror who do you see?
- Do you love the person in the mirror?
- What do you think your eyes convey to others?

Challenge: Stare into the mirror for 3 - 5 minutes. Focus on your eyes. When the time is up, while still looking in the mirror, tell yourself: "I love you". Below, write how it felt telling yourself "I love you".

_____

_____

_____

_____

_____

_____

_____

_____

_____

_____

_____

_____

_____

_____

_____

_____

_____

_____

_____

_____

Day 3: Think Before You Speak

Before you speak, pause and think about what you are going to say.

Peace and harmony can be within us and our families if we learn how to think before we speak. How many times have we accidentally hurt others because the wrong words happened to "slip out"? We have all done it, but of course in the pursuit of change, we want to become aware of our speaking habits.

With discipline and awareness, you will be able to reduce the use of abusive language, which includes fowl language, a yelling and aggressive tone, and words misused through bad intentions.

By changing your speech, your thought process will also change. Your thinking and expression will become more positive if you always use positive words to express yourself. It takes a lot of effort and awareness, but you are on the quest towards change, and this will help you.

THOUGHTS TO CONSIDER

- How often do you use abusive language?
- How many arguments could have been prevented if you would have paused, thought about your ideas, and then spoke to express yourself?

Challenge: Anytime you speak today, pause for 2 seconds, and think about if you whole heartedly mean what you want to say, and then express yourself.

Reflective Questions:

- Why do you use abusive language?
- How did it feel when you paused before speaking?

_____

_____

_____

_____

_____

_____

_____

_____

_____

_____

_____

_____

_____

_____

_____

_____

Day 4: Letting Go of Sadness

Let go of that which causes sadness, pain, and heartache.

Life is full of ups and downs. Deep down we know this, but there are some things from the past that we carry with us throughout our day to day lives which prevents us from feeling any type of peace and joy. It is like a man dragging a very heavy tool across the desert - it takes up all of his energy, he is unable to work, and it does not benefit him.

Letting go of pain and suffering is a scary thought, because you have learned to live and identify with it. You might even be attached to it; however, it is important to remind yourself that you want to change. Letting go of painful thoughts, emotions, experiences, and learning to understand and accept them will liberate you in so many ways. There is no need to hold on to the past which keeps you from enjoying life to its fullest.

It is time to let go.

THOUGHTS TO CONSIDER

- What experiences have made you feel sad for a long time?
- What do you think life would be like if you were not sad?
- How was your health affected as a result of your sadness and pain?
- In what ways did feeling sad hold you back from something?

Challenge: Deeply reflect about 3 factors that have led to sadness in your heart. Write down 5 ways each of these factors have affected your life in a negative way. At the end of this exercise and throughout the day repeat *"I accept (Experience #1, #2, #3) and let it go."*

Experience #1:_____

    1. _____
    2. _____
    3. _____
    4. _____
    5. _____

Experience #2:_____

    1. _____
    2. _____
    3. _____
    4. _____
    5. _____

Experience #3:_____

    1. _____
    2. _____
    3. _____
    4. _____
    5. _____

Day 5: Forgive an Enemy

Think about an enemy, write, and forgive them.

We have all had some negative experiences in our relationships with family, friends, and co-workers. Unfortunately, in rare cases, the relationship is completely lost and we are full of internal anger and hatred towards them.

Feeling anger or hate towards anyone does not benefit anyone at all. Actually, the more you are feeling anger or hate, the more you become mentally and emotionally attached to them. So in the end, the only person who is affected is you.

We need to change this.

Forgiveness is an inner phenomenon. You do not have to wait for someone to apologize or even accept your apology to forgive, because there is a possibility you may not hear from them. But, the whole point of forgiveness is for you to release your negative emotions. Once you forgive the other person, you are actually a freed prisoner, because the only one who was really trapped was you.

THOUGHTS TO CONSIDER

- How often do you think of your "enemy"?
- Why have you been holding on to the hatred or anger for so long?
- What are the benefits of making amends with your enemy?

Challenge: Write a letter to someone who has really hurt you that you have been unable to forgive. Release your thoughts and emotions without holding back. After handwriting your letter, tear it up, or burn it, and throw it in the trash while saying, "I forgive you, I forgive myself for holding it in for so long, and I let it go." Take a deep breath. It is over.

Some ideas to consider when writing your letter:

- Feel the anger, hurt or hatred 100% when writing.
- What did they do to you?
- How did it make you feel?
- Inform them of your forgiveness.

Next, write a few sentences explaining how you felt after your experience with forgiveness.

_____

_____

_____

_____

_____

_____

_____

_____

_____

_____

_____

Day 6: You Are What You Eat

Practice healthy meat-free eating.

There is a saying, "you are what you eat" and it is true. Many are not aware of one reason why we become easily stressed, agitated, angry, and even fearful. Think about what is mainly eaten, meat.

It is very important to be aware of what you eat because what you eat becomes a part of you. Many people have become sick as a result of eating meat that is full of steroids, bacteria, and other diseases. These chemicals are unnatural and do not belong to the human system. You should strive to eat more natural foods such fruits, vegetables, and grains. Simple eating leads to healthy living.

Most of you are probably not vegetarians and that is okay, because you were raised to eat meat. Your family and community probably promoted eating meat – beef, pork, poultry, fish, etc. But, since we are trying new ways to change ourselves towards the better - physically, mentally, and emotionally - what better way to do it than having a meat free day!

THOUGHTS TO CONSIDER

- When you look into animals' eyes, what do you see?
- If you had to hunt and kill for your own food, would you do it?

Challenge: Be meat-free today. Write down the excuses and temptations the mind brings up to convince you to eat meat. Already vegetarian? Write down the experience that helped you change.

Need ideas for vegetarian meals?

- Salads, fruits, vegetables, and grains.
- Most restaurants have vegetarian options.

_____

_____

_____

_____

_____

_____

_____

_____

_____

_____

_____

_____

_____

_____

_____

_____

_____

Day 7: Forget About Forgetting

Remember your tasks with checklists.

With many errands and responsibilities to do each day, it is very easy to forget what needs to be completed. We sometimes go to the grocery store with a specific item in mind to purchase, but once we arrive at the market we buy everything else except the one item we needed. We may also have the procrastination habit of "I'll do it later", but by the end of the evening we have forgotten to do what we were supposed to.

Forgetting very important things can have dire consequences. For example, if your son is left at school and it is your turn to pick him up, he could get lost trying to find his way home. Or, you forget to create an important slide for a business presentation; as a result, you might lose a potential investor.

The excuse of forgetting is often blamed on having too many things to do. Life will be full of "too many things to do" but the key is to learn how to manage, organize, and balance everything that way life becomes less stressful. When we are relaxed, we remember.

THOUGHTS TO CONSIDER

- What was one thing you forgot to do that had bad consequences?
- What are ways you try to organize your "things to do"?
- What cause you to forget?

Challenge: Write down 10 things you need to do today. As you complete each task, place a checkmark next to it or cross it out.

THINGS I MUST COMPLETE TODAY

1. _____
2. _____
3. _____
4. _____
5. _____
6. _____
7. _____
8. _____
9. _____
10. _____

Reflective Questions:

- Knowing that all the above tasks have been completed in an organized way, how does this make you feel?

_____

_____

_____

_____

_____

_____

_____

_____

Weekly Challenge 1: "I Am"

Change yourself; know yourself.

Self-Reflection is the first step towards personal transformation.

To change yourself it is imperative to know what you think of yourself, both the positive and negative. For 30 minutes, write "I am" statements.

For example: "I am trying to change myself."

After 30 minutes of writing "I am" statements, spend 15 minutes reviewing your "I Am" list and mark an asterisk (*) next to the statements that identify the REAL YOU.

I am _____.

I am _____.

I am _____.

I am _____.

I am _____.

I am _____.

I am _____.

I am _____.

I am _____.

I am _____.

I am _____.

I am _____.

I am _____.

I am _____.

I am _____.

I am _____.

I am _____.

I am _____.

I am _____.

I am _____.

I am _____.

I am _____.

I am _____.

Continue on additional sheets of paper.

Day 8: Power of Gratitude

Say Thank You to three people who have changed your life.

Many people come into our lives and make an impact in a positive way. In the moment we are grateful, but as life moves forward these special individuals are either forgotten or have not been remembered in a long time.

Gratitude is a very powerful and humbling experience when it comes from the heart. It is one thing to say "thank you" for receiving a present during the holidays, but it is another to say "thank you" to someone that saved or changed your life; because without them, we would not be who we are today.

In this world, there are only a few people with truly kind, compassionate, and selfless hearts that have given time to help us in our own lives. These special individuals tend to forget what they have done for others because they do not expect anything in return. By saying "thank you", on this random day, their spirits would be lifted, be in positive thoughts, and may even rediscover purpose in their personal life.

THOUGHTS TO CONSIDER

- Who has made a positive and tremendous impact on your life?
- How did they make you a better person?
- What was the situation you were in and how did they help you?

Challenge: Handwrite and mail letters to three individuals that have changed your life in a positive way and say "thank you". Remind them of the situation, how you were feeling, and how they helped or inspired you during that time.

Afterwards, write a few sentences, below, about each of these individuals and why you can never forget them.

1.

_____

_____

_____

_____

_____

2.

_____

_____

_____

_____

_____

3.

_____

_____

_____

_____

_____

Day 9: Childhood Dreams

Reconnect to your inner child's dreams.

We were born with unconditional love, innocence, and a relaxed state of being. Due to conditioning from family, friends, and society during childhood, we have disconnected from our inner self. The child that was care-free, curious, happy, forgiving, and exceptionally pure has become stressed, lost, worried, and extremely tensed as an adult.

Our natural state of being is like that of a baby, completely relaxed, open, and willing to try new things, learn and grow. We knew, as a child, we were different, special, free spirited, and believed anything was possible. It was in these moments we dreamed big and today, it is time to get back to the inner child. The journey to change is backwards.

THOUGHTS TO CONSIDER

- What deep thoughts did you have as a child?
- What did life mean to you while growing up?
- What do you miss most from your childhood?
- What would you like to bring back into your life from your past?
- What did you not like about your childhood?
- What were your childhood dreams?
- Who or what inspired you?

Challenge: Find a few photos or an album from your childhood and look into your eyes. Spend 15 minutes trying to connect to the inner child - what were your thoughts, feelings, and dreams.

Now, take one photo that strikes you, stare at your face, close your eyes, and see yourself as this child. Ask this child only one question: **"Why did I lose you?"** Sit in a relaxed state of silence and listen for the answer. Below, write what your inner child told you.

_____

_____

_____

_____

_____

_____

_____

_____

_____

_____

_____

_____

_____

_____

_____

_____

_____

_____

_____

_____

Day 10: Long Lost Friends

Meet face to face with a long lost friend.

We live in an age of constant interaction through texting, email, and social networking on the internet. However, it is very easy now to miss out on experiencing face to face interaction and communication, which is essential to relationships and friendships. In-person interaction brings a sense of aliveness to both people.

You may have lost touch with someone dear and close to you as a result of family responsibilities, careers, education, moving away, or various other reasons. Maybe you might keep in touch by email or phone, but nothing feels the same as when you greet each other with a warm and loving hug. When reconnecting with one of your long lost friends, you will be able to reminisce on good and happy times in your life, appreciate the friendship more, and experience a special side of yourself that becomes alive when you are around this person. Remember, when in the company of good people you become good.

THOUGHTS TO CONSIDER

- What makes this friend special to you?
- What are some reasons why you have lost touch?
- Will you try and rekindle your friendship?
- What is your primary form of communication with this person?
- What unresolved issues have prevented you from keeping in touch?

Challenge: Call a long lost friend and meet with them face to face today.

Reflective Questions:

- How did it feel speaking with your friend after so many months or years?
- What is the difference when communicating by email or phone versus in person?

_____

_____

_____

_____

_____

_____

_____

_____

_____

_____

_____

_____

_____

_____

Day 11: Dissolving the Prejudice Mind

In public observe your prejudicial thoughts.

We live in an ego-centered world, which essentially means "I am right and you are wrong." This thinking leads to living by stereotypes, labels, disguised prejudice, and ultimately a harmful society. Society would be a much happier place to live in if we all learn to accept one another for who we are, what we believe, how we chose to live our lives, and thereby not superimposing "our way" on others.

Personal change is recognizing our role in this world and how we contribute to the negativity that surrounds us, that way we can improve it. Everyday people are victimized and killed because of their race, culture, gender, sexual orientation, age, and religion, which are a result of prejudice, hatred, and ignorance. Although not publicized, hidden prejudices are fear-based; nonetheless it is something we all have to work on, change, and raise awareness about.

THOUGHTS TO CONSIDER

- Once getting to know someone, how often do you realize your initial perceptions were wrong about that person?
- What does equality mean to you?
- If prejudice and stereotypes were not in this world, how do you think life would be?
- How did it feel being a victim of discrimination?

Challenge: Go to a public area, such as a park, coffee house, mall, parking lot, and observe everyone's actions and speech. Write down the stereotypical and prejudicial thoughts that come into your own mind. Then, remind yourself everyone is equal.

_____

_____

_____

_____

_____

_____

_____

_____

_____

_____

_____

_____

_____

_____

_____

_____

_____

_____

_____

_____

_____

Day 12: Anger Awareness

Be aware and anger will leave you.

Anger affects our lives on a daily basis although we may not even notice it. The reaction has become natural to us; we believe it is us.

Anger is something that is separate from you, but unfortunately controls you. It is a very strong emotion that often causes a physical response such as stress, frustration, yelling, violence, high blood pressure, and stubbornness.

The misconception about working on anger is the need to control it. The way to dissolve anger is to become aware of it. You break a destructive cycle which leads to mental, emotional, and physical pain by acknowledging your anger. Awareness will have a lesser affect on you and you will less likely react to it. Increasing awareness of anger means your anger may last two minutes instead of two days.

THOUGHTS TO CONSIDER

- How do you express your anger positively and negatively?
- What makes you angry and violent?
- Do you feel in control or does anger control you?
- How do you try to calm yourself down when angry?

Challenge: Watch yourself today and instantly become aware when you become angry, stressed, or frustrated. As soon as you become aware, take 3 deep breaths, drink a glass of cold water, and remind yourself, "I am not my anger."

Reflective Questions:

- How many times did you get angry today?
- Was it easier to remain calm when you became aware?
- How does practicing awareness during an angry episode make you feel?

_____

_____

_____

_____

_____

_____

_____

_____

_____

_____

_____

_____

_____

_____

Day 13: Public Speaking

Speak your mind, speak your heart.

Public Speaking is one of the most feared things to do - to get up in front of a crowd and speak from your heart and mind. It is one thing to be able to give a presentation for business or deliver lectures if it is your job and you are accustomed to it, but it is a different story if you speak about something that is very close to your heart, that you are passionate, sensitive about, and wish to express yourself to others.

The quivering voice, the shaky knees, and the cold hands are a result of nervousness and fear because there is a lack of self confidence. So many times actors accept an award on stage and are nervous to speak because they are without a script or prior coaching.

For some, it is easier to speak to a large crowd of strangers than speak to their own family and friends. To help boost self confidence in your communication and self-expression, you will speak your mind and heart today.

THOUGHTS TO CONSIDER

- What makes you nervous about public or private speaking?
- What does self-confidence mean to you? Do you have it?
- What emotions do you find hard to express in public?
- What judgmental thoughts of others do you fear most?

Challenge: Invite 1 – 5 family members or friends over to your home. Before they arrive, reflect on a topic that you are passionate about. For 10 minutes, stand up in front of them and speak. Some helpful tips include taking a deep breath right before speaking and stretching.

Reflective Questions:

- Why did you select your topic?
- How did public speaking feel once you were finished?
- What self-conscious thoughts did you experience?

_____

_____

_____

_____

_____

_____

_____

_____

_____

_____

_____

_____

_____

_____

_____

_____

Day 14: Eat Together

As a family, eat together in peace.

Connecting together as a family, sitting at a table, and engaging in quality conversation is often missing during family meals because of different schedules, priorities, work at home, and many other reasons. When families communicate in peace during meals it brings unity and closeness to the family. Mealtime is a perfect opportunity to discuss ideas, ask questions of each other, deepen relationships, and sincerely connect with each other while forgetting the stress of daily life.

Eating at different times, with one person eating at the table, one in the office, another in front of the television and another out at a restaurant does not help the family system stay united and close. Try once a week to get the family to be of help to each other during dinner time. One can setup the table while another cooks. Once the meal is finished someone else can wash the dishes and put the food away. Setting aside a time to sit together in peace, with family communication as the main focus, will change your life and those in your family.

THOUGHTS TO CONSIDER

- How often does the family sit together to enjoy a meal?
- What would benefit you if you ate with your family?
- When you eat, do you eat with love and peace?
- How often do you spend time with your family daily?

Challenge: Sit and eat together as a family for at least an hour. Set aside a specific time, setup the dinner table like a formal dinner, and eat together in peace.

Before the meal starts, tell each of your family members present at the table you love them, are grateful to them in your life, and why.

Describe how it felt to eat together as a family.

_____

_____

_____

_____

_____

_____

_____

_____

_____

_____

_____

_____

_____

_____

_____

_____

_____

Weekly Challenge 2: Life's Purpose

Discover your life's purpose.

Life's purpose is the very reason for your existence.

Challenge: Take 20 minutes to reflect and write down what you feel your life's purposes are.

Reflective Questions:

- Why do you exist?
- What does life mean to you?

_____

_____

_____

_____

_____

_____

_____

_____

_____

_____

_____

_____

_____

_____

_____

_____

_____

_____

_____

_____

_____

_____

_____

_____

_____

_____

_____

_____

_____

_____

_____

_____

_____

_____

Day 15: Clean Living

Clean your living space.

Living in a clean environment keeps a person healthy, organized, and in pure thoughts. A clean home also brings peace and calmness into one's life.

You should clean your home in detail at least 3 – 4 times a year on top of your weekly house cleaning. Taking care of your home, less dust and bacteria will accumulate, thus reducing the possibilities of getting sick. The main areas of your home that should be cleaned weekly are your kitchen, bathroom and sleeping space, since these are the most used areas. Weekly cleaning should include sweeping, mopping, vacuuming, and scrubbing all surfaces.

Daily, you should always clean your stove, wash your dishes, and wipe your kitchen and bathroom counters dry after use.

THOUGHTS TO CONSIDER

- How does cleaning make you feel?
- How often do you clean?
- What prevents you from cleaning daily?
- How do you think cleaning will benefit you and your family?

Challenge: Clean your home. Ensure all of the following are completed.

Kitchen Area:

- Wash your dishes and put them on the shelf
- Scrub and wash your sink
- Wash and clean your stove
- Clean your microwave
- Sweep and mop the floor
- Wipe all counter and cupboard surfaces
- Take out the trash

Bathroom Area:

- Scrub and clean your toilet
- Scrub and clean your bathtub/shower
- Scrub and wash your sink
- Wipe your mirrors
- Sweep and mop the floor
- Take out the trash

Living and Sleeping Space:

- Wipe down with a wet cloth all surfaces to remove dust
- Sweep, mop and vacuum
- Make your bed
- Wipe all door knobs in your home with soap and water
- Take out the trash

Day 16: Fasting for Health

Fast for one meal.

Fasting is a healthy form of cleansing the body of toxins and negativities. Fasting also breaks one of the human being's greatest habits, over-eating. Eating food is necessary to survive, but most do not eat in moderation and eat only because a meal tastes good.

At this time, there is a worldwide concern for obesity and unhealthy eating. Obesity is the result of lack of knowledge, discipline, and self-awareness. Although some may not be obese, some obsess over food as a form of comfort. Relying on food to make you happy is not healthy for the body and mind. Food is not a requirement for happiness nor should it be an addiction.

There are many ways of fasting such as fruit fasts, juice fasts, and water fasts. Depending on your body, you might consider a short fast, like fasting for one meal, which will be beneficial for your health.

THOUGHTS TO CONSIDER

- What have you heard about fasting?
- How do you think it will benefit you?
- Are you addicted to food?
- Do you eat in moderation?
- Have you ever become sick as a result of over-eating?

Challenge: Fast for one meal today. Drink water or juice instead of eating an entire meal.

Consult a medical expert to ensure this one-meal fast will not affect your current health or strict diet. You may experience a slight headache or minor light-headedness, depending on your body type.

Reflective Questions:

- Describe what your mind and body are feeling during your one meal fast?
- How does fasting with health-awareness feel?

_____

_____

_____

_____

_____

_____

_____

_____

_____

_____

_____

_____

_____

_____

_____

Day 17: Soft Talk

Avoid yelling at your family, colleagues, or children.

We have all taken our problems and frustrations out on those who are closest to us. Even though the other person may not be the cause of our issues, we still yell and scream at them as if it is their fault. We need to become aware of the consequences of our actions in order to prevent someone from getting hurt.

Maybe you are juggling a lot of things in your life your family, work, school, time management, and so much more. When things do not go your way or there is not enough time to complete all of your tasks, it is very understandable that you might get frustrated; however, it is neither fair nor right for someone to be yelled at just because you are stressed out.

Everyone can detect the frustration in another's voice. We hear it in their tone, pitch, and volume. When we respond in a discussion with yelling, the other person may yell too, resulting in an unnecessary argument which is "added to the list of problems" for the day. Use a calm voice creating more peace in your life and relationships.

THOUGHTS TO CONSIDER

- How do you feel when you yell at others out of frustration?
- What do you accomplish by yelling?
- What often triggers you to yell at others?

Challenge: When speaking with your family, friends, co-workers, or children today, do not yell or use an aggressive tone, regardless of how frustrated or stressed out you are. Count how many arguments you avoid by speaking with a friendly, calm, and soft voice.

Reflective Questions:

- How does it feel to speak with a calm voice?
- How does it feel to not be confrontational or competitive?

_____

_____

_____

_____

_____

_____

_____

_____

_____

_____

_____

_____

_____

_____

_____

_____

Day 18: Love Thy Pet

Be affectionate towards your pets and all animals.

Nature is full of wonderful animals which serve a purpose and bring balance to our earth. Some animals have become our best friends because they live in our homes, work at our farms, or are just so beautiful to observe when we are walking out in nature.

Because of the daily responsibilities in life, we often forget to give animals love and affection. Feeding animals and taking them outside to relieve themselves does not count as love. Fulfilling your duties is different than holding, talking to, and petting the animals. Remember, all animals want to be loved just as humans do.

Whether it is a tarantula spider, turtle, hamster, dog, cat, or horse, all pets need tender loving care. By spending even a few moments with them daily, they become very happy, feel the love, and enjoy being who they are. They are appreciated as they should be.

THOUGHTS TO CONSIDER

- How often do you play with your pets?
- How have animals benefited your life?
- What signs do animals give you to catch your attention?
- What purpose do animals serve in your life?
- In what ways do you show animals you love them?

Challenge: Spend 15 minutes of quality time with your pet. Talk to, pet and hold them. Through instinct they will feel your friendly and loving gestures.

Don't have any pets?

- Visit a local pet store and spend time petting some animals.
- Go to a beach or local park and ask to pet another's dog.
- Sit outside and watch all the birds, listen to them sing.
- Visit a local animal shelter, they'd love the attention!

Reflective Questions:

- How does it feel to show affection to your pets and animals?
- How do animals respond to your love?

_____

_____

_____

_____

_____

_____

_____

_____

_____

_____

_____

_____

Day 19: Save the Planet

Protect the planet, recycle.

We protect and clean our homes, but our planet needs our attention, too. On the streets of our cities, the sands of the beach and in our oceans trash is spread everywhere. Every piece of trash that we throw out the window or off to the side while walking is contributing towards the pollution of our planet.

The planet should be treated as our home. We need to clean, care for, and respect it because it protects our survival. If we live in a world completely full of pollution and trash, our lungs will be filled with bacteria, there would not be any pure oxygen, and our water supply would be tainted, and thus we could not survive as a human race.

You may not be able to save the whole planet, but you can do your part. You can always separate your own trash at home and put recyclable items into a separate bin. Some cities provide this through local recycling centers. Save your cans and recycle them. Throwing away your trash in the right place helps the community.

THOUGHTS TO CONSIDER

- How often do you separate your recyclable items from normal trash?
- In what ways do you help the earth and what ways do you pollute it?

Challenge: Be active today in helping the environment. Pick up at least 20 pieces of trash in public and put it in the garbage or recycling bins. It is a humbling experience to help the community and be an example to others.

Reflective Questions:

- In what ways do you plan to help reduce pollution?

_____

_____

_____

_____

_____

_____

_____

_____

_____

_____

_____

_____

_____

_____

_____

_____

_____

Day 20: Breathe in Nature

Breathe in. Breathe out.

Breathing is natural and therefore it should be relaxed. We live in a tense world, which is reflected in our breathing. When we are angry and aggressive, our breathing is very fast and labored. When we are excited and hyper, our breathing is rapid and shallow. When relaxed, our breathing is full, calm, and expanded. We need to return back to our natural relaxed state, like a baby.

Babies are perfect examples of our natural state that we have lost. When we see babies sleeping, they are peaceful and innocent. If we focus on the baby's breathing we notice they have a full breath which begins at the belly and expands to the chest. It is important to practice deep and full breaths to maintain our health and calmness.

Practicing full breaths outside in nature allows you to fill and expand your lungs with pure oxygen. Being outside, you are also away from situations that keep you anxious, worried, stressed, or angry. Nature is healing, your breath is natural. Breathing can heal you.

THOUGHTS TO CONSIDER

- How often do you notice your own breath?
- What are your experiences of practicing breath awareness?
- What makes your breathing shallow or fast?

Challenge: Go outside for fresh air and take 5 deep breaths. Inhale for 5 seconds, hold your breath for 5 seconds, and then exhale for 5 seconds. Repeat this exercise for 2 minutes.

Write down how you feel after your deep breathing exercise. Contemplate how this deep breathing can change your life when you are stressed or tensed.

_____

_____

_____

_____

_____

_____

_____

_____

_____

_____

_____

_____

_____

_____

_____

_____

_____

_____

Day 21: Know your World

Know what is happening in the world you live in.

In every moment there is something happening in our world community. Although we cannot stay up to date with the entire world's adventures and afflictions, at minimum we can spend a few minutes a day to know what is happening. It is important to stay engaged because we learn what is occurring in our neighborhoods, government, and in other nations, therefore we can make sound decisions on how to protect ourselves, vote, and be informed.

We may all have our opinions about the news and media, and some of us may or may not trust our sources; however, it is still imperative to know what is currently happening in society because we are affected by it somehow.

There are several ways of discovering what is taking place today, such as: local or cable news, newspapers, magazines, rss feeds, blogs, and online social networking websites.

THOUGHTS TO CONSIDER

- How do you keep up with local and world news?
- Why do you think it is important to be engaged in news?
- What are the advantages of knowing what is happening today?
- How does news affect you?
- Are you too attached to news?

Challenge: Spend 15 minutes today watching or reading local and world news. List 5 things that happened today and how it made you feel.

Story #1:

_____

_____

Story #2:

_____

_____

Story #3:

_____

_____

Story #4:

_____

_____

Story #5:

_____

_____

Weekly Challenge 3: Fears

Identify your fears.

Fear is an instinctive feeling to protect ourselves where there is a threat, if we are to lose something, experience pain, or die. There is nothing to fear, if we truly understand and accept our own death.

Although some of us may continue to fear death, it is also important to work on the fears that are easier to face and overcome. Any fear should not stop you from being yourself, doing what you love, or cause you stress. Where there is fear, *you* disappear.

Challenge: Identify your fears, why you fear, and steps to overcome them.

_____

_____

_____

_____

_____

_____

_____

_____

_____

_____

_____

_____

_____

_____

_____

_____

_____

_____

_____

_____

_____

_____

_____

_____

_____

_____

_____

_____

_____

_____

_____

_____

_____

_____

_____

Day 22: Breaking Habits

Avoid smoking, drinking, gambling, or taking illegal drugs.

Although smoking cigarettes, drinking alcohol, and taking drugs are somehow acceptable in society, it is not healthy for you emotionally, mentally, and physically. We know all these things, "Don't smoke," "Don't drink and drive," and "Don't do drugs" yet still do it.

Change does not happen overnight and neither does quitting bad habits; however, like committing to taking these challenges, you should also be disciplined in avoiding bad habits that you know are not good for you. Smoking, alcohol, and drugs kill. Why do you do it?

Maybe smoking, drinking, or doing drugs may not be your habits, but I am sure you can find a few things that you do in your life that are not healthy for you that you know deep down you would like to stop. Let today be that day to drop at least one bad habit.

THOUGHTS TO CONSIDER

- What are the benefits of smoking, drinking, gambling, and drugs?
- What bad habits do you possess that you would like to quit?
- Although fatal, why do people keep these types of habits?
- How do you feel when you are performing your bad habit?

Challenge: Do not smoke, drink, gamble, take illegal drugs, or perform any unhealthy habits today. Resist the emotional, mental, and physical urge. Take control of your life. Write down, after the day is over, how it felt to resist unhealthy habit temptations.

_____

_____

_____

_____

_____

_____

_____

_____

_____

_____

_____

_____

_____

_____

_____

_____

_____

_____

_____

_____

_____

Day 23: Non-Violence

Refrain from hitting, throwing, and screaming.

Some of us have learned to express our anger and frustrations through violence, such as hitting, throwing objects, and uncontrollable screaming. Although sometimes such acts of violence are unintentional and done "in the moment", it is important not to create a bad habit out of it; because it may go too far and someone may get hurt – mentally, emotionally, and physically – or even killed.

Many men, women, and children are victims of domestic violence. It first starts as an "in the moment" first offense and later it becomes habitual. We need to protect ourselves from such abuse and also be aware not to abuse others. If we learn to express our emotions and thoughts nonviolently, there is more possibility for conflict resolution and management through communication.

If you learn to be nonviolent you will change immediately.

THOUGHTS TO CONSIDER

- How does it feel to hurt someone you care for?
- What do you gain from doing such violent actions?
- What are other negative ways you express yourself?
- How do you express yourself when angry or emotional?
- How do you practice nonviolence in your life?

Challenge: Do not hit, throw, or scream at anyone today. Instead, if any type of emotion arises, go for a walk outside and do not return unless you have completely calmed down.

Write down positive ways you can manage or respond to conflict.

_____

_____

_____

_____

_____

_____

_____

_____

_____

_____

_____

_____

_____

_____

_____

_____

_____

Day 24: Time to Stretch

Be healthy and stretch.

Stretching is a great way to relieve stress and stay flexible. After waking up, long hours of sitting, or even after working, it is a good idea to get the blood flowing in your body. Increased blood flow reduces tension in the muscles thereby allowing you to relax.

Yoga is one way to stretch and stay physically healthy. The practice is becoming more popular as studios are in most major cities; however, even reaching your arms over your head, twisting your body from side to side, or sitting on the floor with legs straight and reaching for your toes are helpful. It only takes a few minutes a day to stretch, why not do it?

If we observe animals, they are usually relaxed and natural. When a dog wakes up in the morning he first stretches and gets ready to play for the day. Stretching on a daily basis creates flexibility and relieves stress - stretching with intense breathing can be healing.

THOUGHTS TO CONSIDER

- How often do you stretch?
- What are your thoughts about yoga?
- What other forms of exercise do you do daily or weekly?

Challenge: Stretch for 10 - 20 minutes today. Begin and end your stretch time with 5 deep breaths. Use stretching exercises that you are most comfortable with and know. Try not to overdo it; instead, relax while you stretch.

If you are familiar with yoga or wish to research and try some postures, use the following simple asanas. Easy to follow instructions are available at *YogaJournal.com.*

- Standing Forward Bend (uttanasana)
- Standing Back Bend (anuvittasana)
- Triangle Pose (trikonasana)
- Warrior Pose (virabhadrasana)
- Legs Wide Forward Bend (prasarita padottanasana)
- Downward Dog (adho mukha svanasana)
- Child Pose (balasana)
- Seated Forward Bend (paschimottanasana)
- Cobra Pose (bhujangasana)
- Jog / Run in Place

Reflective Questions:

- How often can you commit to stretching each day?
- How did stretching make you feel?

_____

_____

_____

_____

_____

Day 25: Saving Money

Set aside cash for emergencies.

Saving money is difficult to do when hard economic times hit. Nonetheless, we should always set aside at minimum $5 from every weekly paycheck we receive. That is an emergency savings of $260 each year. The amount of savings will increase if we save more than $5 per week.

Getting in the habit of saving will benefit you in that it will ease the stress when an emergency happens because you will always know you have a little extra cash saved. It is up to you if you wish to put your savings in a bank account or hidden box somewhere in your home, but the most important thing is that you save.

We all need to learn how to save and become less stressed. It is very important for all of us to be prepared for anything to happen because a tragedy can strike any day as a result of the economy, weather, or politics that we have no control over.

By saving money now, you save yourself in the future.

THOUGHTS TO CONSIDER

- How would you feel knowing you have a little extra savings?
- How much do you think you can set aside from each check?
- Why have you not saved much before?

Challenge: Deposit $20 - $100 into your savings account today, or put this amount in a box, preferably with a lock, that you can safely place and hide in your home.

Starting today, how much will you be depositing into your savings box each week?

$_____

Write down the location of the box in case you forget where you placed it:

_____

List other ways you can start saving money:

_____

_____

_____

_____

_____

_____

_____

_____

_____

_____

_____

_____

Day 26: Absence of Criticism

Abstain from criticizing others in your thoughts and words.

We are equal. No one is better or less than anyone. Yes, we are all unique and different, but we are all equal. Criticism of others is rooted in the idea that we are superior to others. We criticize someone's good works because we think we can do a better job or because we are envious. We disapprove of those that do not meet our standards because they are not like us. We criticize others because in our minds the other is always wrong. We criticize because we are insecure with ourselves. Criticism towards others should be ceased. We should criticize ourselves and be aware of our own shortcomings first, before criticizing others for theirs.

Change means focusing on yourself first. Find your weaknesses, be aware of your habits, and then work on them. You will have your weaknesses and others will, too. But, it is imperative to understand that the only person you can change is yourself. Criticizing others does no good except to reveal how weak you are.

Self-Criticism allows you to see the higher qualities in others and helps you to realize your lower qualities that need attention and work. It is the best criticism, because in the end you are the one to change and make yourself a better individual.

THOUGHTS TO CONSIDER

- What are your weaknesses and lower qualities?
- What makes you think you are superior to others?

Challenge: Do not think or speak a word of criticism to anyone today.

Reflective Questions:

- Why do you criticize others?
- What makes you feel superior and inferior to others?
- What does self-criticism mean to you?

_____

_____

_____

_____

_____

_____

_____

_____

_____

_____

_____

_____

Day 27: Living in the Present Moment

The past and future of the mind causes suffering; live in the present.

Our mind is constantly running and bouncing between the past and future. Dwelling in the past causes us to suffer and dreaming about the future keeps us anxious and worried. The past is gone and the future never comes, both options are out of our hands. When we let go of the past and future, we learn to live in the present moment.

Living in the present moment means to put your whole heart, mind, and being into whatever you are doing at present. There is no room for thoughts about the past and future because you are completely focused. For example, a college student can be present and at the same time he is absent. Meaning, if the student was really present, he would be learning and absorbing everything the teacher says, instead of absent as a result of his wandering mind about last night's party.

The more you realize you are living in the past and future and begin to live in the present, the more you will be able to experience calmness, peace, and real happiness.

THOUGHTS TO CONSIDER

- How often do you live in the present moment?
- What does it feel like when you are not thinking about the past and future?

Challenge: At every hour today (8:00am, 9:00am, etc.) close your eyes, perform 30 seconds of deep breathing, relax for a moment, and then continue working. Pausing, even for a few seconds, helps us return to the present moment to just relax and be.

Write down ways you can live in the present moment.

_____

_____

_____

_____

_____

_____

_____

_____

_____

_____

_____

_____

_____

_____

_____

_____

_____

_____

_____

Day 28: Trusting the Inner Me

Listen to the inner voice and learn to trust it.

Trust is a very important factor in any form of relationship. Trust is earned and it is not a privilege. It is important to understand that we must first learn to trust ourselves before trying to trust others. Developing trust in ourselves, we learn to be confident and validate our own lives, instead of relying on others.

Know your strengths, weaknesses, and the nature of your own mind. When you know yourself you will be able to know others.

One way to develop trust is listening to the gut and instinctive feeling that arises within you and acting upon it. Animals are very instinctive; however, humans have lost their instincts because the mind likes to play tricks, cause doubt, fear, or confusion.

You need to increase your ability to listen to the inner voice, and know the difference between the mind and the real voice before trust takes place. After time, you will go beyond trust and just "know".

THOUGHTS TO CONSIDER

- How often do you rely on your inner voice?
- Why do you not trust yourself?
- What prevents you from trusting others?

Challenge: Write down 5 reasons why people trust you and 5 reasons why they should not trust you.

_____   _____

_____   _____

_____   _____

_____   _____

_____   _____

Reflective Questions:

- What is it about their reasoning for trusting you that you be-lieve or not believe about yourself?
- What can you do to improve the 5 reasons why others cannot trust you?

_____

_____

_____

_____

_____

_____

_____

_____

_____

Weekly Challenge 4: Achievements

Know what you want, and go get it.

Life should be full of achievements – whether big or small. Anything can become an achievement, because you know what you want and then you put effort to achieve it.

THOUGHTS TO CONSIDER:

- What does success mean to you?
- What are your past achievements?

Challenge: Reflect for 20 minutes and list what you would like to achieve in your life, why it is important to you and your first step to help you reach your destination.

_____

_____

_____

_____

_____

_____

_____

_____

Day 29: Personal Confessions

Share your secrets with nature.

We all have our own secrets, regrets, negative emotions, and guilt for something we have said, thought, or done. We are afraid to reveal these secrets to anyone because of our fears, it may cause harm or it is just not necessary to declare. However, there is internal harm being done to us because it has not been released from our mind. Holding something inside of us for so long can make a person mentally, emotionally, and physically sick. We are striving for peace of mind, a step towards overcoming our past transgressions.

Releasing your deep dark secrets, regrets, negative emotions, and guilt will be beneficial for you. It is not necessary that you have to say any of it to a specific person or out in public, but by just speaking it out loud in nature inner healing can happen.

Nature sees and hears all. Nature can be your best friend because you can talk, connect, and love it and in return it always listens and accepts anything you say. Communicating with nature can release many feelings that you have kept inside that has caused pain, sadness, anger, and guilt.

THOUGHTS TO CONSIDER

- What negative feelings or secrets do you have that keep you from inner peace and happiness?

Challenge: Find a safe spot at a beach, community park, in your own backyard or garden. Speak to the ocean, tree, or flower. Spend 30 minutes to 1 hour connecting and communicating with nature. Say out loud any and all secrets, feelings of guilt, negative emotions, or regrets that you may have kept deep inside yourself for a long time. Do not hold back. Remember, nature does not judge, it just loves and listens.

Reflective Questions:

- How did it feel to release all the thoughts and emotions that were built up inside of you?
- What feelings were you able to release?
- What immediate change did you feel when speaking to nature?
- What did nature say back to you?

_____

_____

_____

_____

_____

_____

_____

_____

_____

_____

_____

Day 30: Changing Together

Write a letter and describe how you have changed.

We have taken this journey together towards change and it would be an honor to hear from you and your story of personal change. It is an inspiration to me to know that you have taken up these difficult life changing challenges, put efforts towards improving your life, and thus changing the world.

The journey of change can be frightening and liberating, but it does not have to be lonely. Know that I am here to listen and believe in you.

THOUGHTS TO CONSIDER

- How has this 31 Day Challenge changed your life?
- What aspects have you decided you would like to improve on more?
- Which challenge was the most difficult and why?
- How do you feel after changing certain aspects of your life?
- What challenge was the easiest and why?
- Describe how it feels to have been in discipline for the past 4 weeks?
- What have you learned about yourself?
- How do you see yourself today from when you first started?

Challenge: Write and mail a letter answering the following questions:

- What inspired you to take a step towards change?
- How have you changed as a result of your efforts?
- Which challenge changed you the most?
- What are your plans to continue your journey to change?

Be sure to include your name, mailing address and email address.

If you would like to, include a photo of yourself and your family. If you wish to remain anonymous that is okay, too!

Mail your letter to:

Change Challenge #30
C/O Sadhvi Siddhali Shree
9985 E. Hwy 56
Windom, Texas, 75492 USA

Reflect and write about how these challenges changed your life.

_____

_____

_____

_____

_____

_____

_____

_____

_____

Day 31: The Next 31 Days

Prepare for the next 31 days of challenges.

Taking a step towards change, such as completing these challenges, is just the beginning towards personal transformation. Every New Year we also want to change something about us, but without direction or discipline we give up after the first few days. Then, we wait until the next year to try to attempt change again.

By coming this far, you have proven to yourself that you have the tenacity, courage, and will-power to change. Do not let today be your last day of your journey towards change, let it be the start of a better and new life.

Remember the 31 ways you listed on your very first day of the challenges? It may seem like you were a different person and it was so long ago, but now it is time to go back to where you were, reflect, and prepare for your next 31 days of challenge.

THOUGHTS TO CONSIDER

- What specific challenges did you like in this book?
- What specific challenges did you not like?
- How do you feel knowing you committed to change, and changed?
- In what ways would you like to change, aside from the areas you listed on your first day?

Challenge: You will setup your own personal *31 Day Challenge to a Changed You*. Follow the steps in order.

1. Get 31 pieces of notebook/computer paper.
2. Write down on each sheet of a paper one of the changes you listed on Day 1's challenge.
3. Under each change you listed on each sheet of paper, write down a specific action you can do that will help you meet that change.
4. Fold each sheet of paper four times.
5. Place all 31 folded pieces of paper into a box or bag.
6. Place this box or bag somewhere you will not forget to check daily.
7. Each day, go to your "Change Box" and pick out one piece of paper.
8. Perform the challenge you select every day.
9. When the "Change Box" is empty, return to this page and repeat the steps. Or, create a new list of 31 day changes with new specific and practical challenges to perform.

Sample of Sheets:

Change: (*what you want to change*) Action: (*a step towards that change*)
Change: I want to reduce my stress. Action: I will practice deep breathing for 30 seconds when I feel stressed.

It's Only the Beginning

If you have completed this intensive 31 Day Challenge, you have changed your life in some way. I am very proud of you and you should be proud of yourself, too. I am sure some of the challenges were not easy for you, but like all great achievements, determination, discipline, and effort are required. Your present achievement - *A Changed You.*

Change is constant and never ends. There will always be aspects of your life that need constant awareness, attention, and action. If you need to repeat this guide over and over again to keep you in a disciplined routine, then do it. If you only wish to repeat or expand only certain challenges, go for it. Your efforts towards personal transformation should never cease because there is always room for growth.

This book was only a first step on your life's journey. It is with hope you have learned to love, believe, have confidence, and trust in yourself, because I love, believe, have confidence, and put my trust in **you**.

Continue to grow, ask self reflective questions, and seek out the truth that is within you. Find, discover, and know yourself. By this alone, you have changed the world.

About the Author

Sadhvi Siddhali Shree is a spiritual monk and the Spiritual Director of Siddhayatan Spiritual Retreat, near Dallas, Texas.

Siddhali Shree lost her mother to cancer when she was thirteen. It was because of this tragedy she began her spiritual path four years later when she accepted her mother's death. A high school teacher helped Siddhali Shree begin to believe, find, and change herself. It was in this crucial time she started to self reflect, question, and begin the quest to finding purpose and hope in her own life.

Although spiritually inclined at a young age, Siddhali Shree felt it was her duty to serve in the United States Army. In 2004, after initially meeting Acharya Shree Yogeesh, her spiritual teacher, she voluntarily deployed to Iraq as a Combat Medic Sergeant. After seeing firsthand the effects of war and violence, Siddhali Shree felt more determined to bring peace to the world. Upon her return from a 16 month deployment, Siddhali Shree completed her Communication B. A. in 2½ years at California State University, Long Beach.

Siddhali Shree's goal, as a spiritual teacher, is to bring the messages of non-violence, peace, compassion, and spirituality to today's world. She believes that the current society is in the grip of materialism, consumerism, violence, sex, and drugs promoted by the media and government, and thus lacking in spirituality. Her goals are to encourage children and young adults to learn and incorporate spiritual values into their lives, empower women, and create balance in a male-oriented society.

Sadhvi Siddhali Shree

Acknowledgments

Acharya Shree Yogeesh, my humble gratitude for your continued spiritual guidance, inspiration, and wisdom. Thank you for having confidence in my abilities and me.

Ms. R., thank you for being my first spiritual teacher. For without your patience and faith in me when I was seventeen, I would not be where I am today.

Fayvor, thank you for your time, efforts, ideas, and editing. I have every confidence in you, your purpose, and visions for this world.

Riddhika, thank you for your help in editing this book. I am continually grateful for your support in my new ideas and endeavors. You truly reflect your spiritual name, you are a treasure.

Thank you to all readers of this book, for challenging and changing yourself and consequently, changing the world.

Recommended Resources

Hidden Treasures of the Soul: A Spiritual Blog
http://SiddhaliShree.com

Siddhayatan Spiritual Retreat Center – Dallas, Texas
http://Siddhayatan.org
9985 E. Hwy 56
Windom, Texas, 75492
Info@Siddhayatan.org

Yogeesh Ashram
http://YogeeshAshram.org
16345 Whispering Spur St.
Riverside, California, 92504

YouTube, Inc. Channels
http://YouTube.com/SiddhaliShree
http://YouTube.com/YogeeshAshram

Siddha Sangh Publications
http://SiddhaSanghPublications.com
9985 E. Hwy 56
Windom, Texas, 75492

Contact the Author
Sadhvi Siddhali Shree
SiddhaliShree@Siddhayatan.org

Siddha Sangh Publications

Secrets of Enlightenment, Volume I   **$15.00**
By Dr. Acharya Shree Yogeesh
A collection of spiritual discourses from 2002-2004.

Secrets of Enlightenment, Volume II   **$15.00**
By Dr. Acharya Shree Yogeesh
A collection of spiritual discourses from 2004-2006.

Mail order and payment to:
Siddha Sangh Publications, 9985 E. Hwy 56, Windom, Texas, 75492

= =

NAME:_____

ADDRESS:_____

CITY: _____

STATE:_____ ZIP CODE:_____

COUNTRY:_____

Secrets of Enlightenment, Vol. I   Quantity_____
Secrets of Enlightenment, Vol. II   Quantity_____

Include $5.00 shipping/handling per book.

www.ingramcontent.com/pod-product-compliance
Lightning Source LLC
Chambersburg PA
CBHW060405050426
42449CB00009B/1911